FATH

DATE:

TODAY I WANT TO SAY TO MY DAUGHTER

_____
_____
_____
_____

WHAT MY DAUGHTER DID TODAY AND (WHY) IT MADE ME PROUD/HAPPY/ SURPRISED/UPSET

_____
_____
_____
_____
_____

MY ADVICE TO MY DAUGHTER

_____
_____

I WANT TO DO WITH MY DAUGHTER

_____
_____
_____
_____

DAUGHTER

DATE: _____

TODAY I WANT TO SAY TO MY DAD

_____

_____

_____

_____

WHAT MY DAD DID TODAY AND (WHY) IT MADE ME PROUD/HAPPY/ SURPRISED/UPSET

_____

_____

_____

_____

_____

MY ADVICE TO MY DAD

_____

I WANT TO DO WITH MY DAD

_____

_____

_____

_____

FATHER

DATE:

TODAY I WANT TO SAY TO MY DAUGHTER

_____
_____
_____
_____
_____

WHAT MY DAUGHTER DID TODAY AND (WHY) IT MADE ME PROUD/HAPPY/ SURPRISED/UPSET

_____
_____
_____
_____
_____

MY ADVICE TO MY DAUGHTER

_____
_____

I WANT TO DO WITH MY DAUGHTER

_____
_____
_____

DAUGHTER

DATE: _____

TODAY I WANT TO SAY TO MY DAD

_____

_____

_____

_____

_____

WHAT MY DAD DID TODAY AND (WHY) IT MADE ME PROUD/HAPPY/ SURPRISED/UPSET

_____

_____

_____

_____

_____

MY ADVICE TO MY DAD

_____

_____

I WANT TO DO WITH MY DAD

_____

_____

_____

_____

FATHER

DATE:

TODAY I WANT TO SAY TO MY DAUGHTER

_____
_____
_____
_____
_____
_____

WHAT MY DAUGHTER DID TODAY AND (WHY) IT MADE ME PROUD/HAPPY/ SURPRISED/UPSET

_____
_____
_____
_____
_____
_____

MY ADVICE TO MY DAUGHTER

_____
_____

I WANT TO DO WITH MY DAUGHTER

_____
_____
_____
_____

DAUGHTER

DATE:

TODAY I WANT TO SAY TO MY DAD

_____

_____

_____

_____

WHAT MY DAD DID TODAY AND (WHY) IT MADE ME PROUD/HAPPY/ SURPRISED/UPSET

_____

_____

_____

_____

MY ADVICE TO MY DAD

_____

_____

I WANT TO DO WITH MY DAD

_____

_____

_____

_____

FATHER

DATE:

TODAY I WANT TO SAY TO MY DAUGHTER

_____
_____
_____
_____
_____

WHAT MY DAUGHTER DID TODAY AND (WHY) IT MADE ME PROUD/HAPPY/ SURPRISED/UPSET

_____
_____
_____
_____
_____

MY ADVICE TO MY DAUGHTER

_____
_____

I WANT TO DO WITH MY DAUGHTER

_____
_____
_____
_____

DAUGHTER

DATE:

TODAY I WANT TO SAY TO MY DAD

_____
_____
_____
_____
_____

WHAT MY DAD DID TODAY AND (WHY) IT MADE ME PROUD/HAPPY/ SURPRISED/UPSET

_____
_____
_____
_____
_____

MY ADVICE TO MY DAD

_____
_____
_____

I WANT TO DO WITH MY DAD

_____
_____
_____
_____

FATHER

DATE:

TODAY I WANT TO SAY TO MY DAUGHTER

_____

_____

_____

_____

_____

WHAT MY DAUGHTER DID TODAY AND (WHY) IT MADE ME PROUD/HAPPY/ SURPRISED/UPSET

_____

_____

_____

_____

_____

_____

MY ADVICE TO MY DAUGHTER

_____

_____

I WANT TO DO WITH MY DAUGHTER

_____

_____

_____

_____

DAUGHTER

DATE: _____

TODAY I WANT TO SAY TO MY DAD

_____

_____

_____

_____

_____

WHAT MY DAD DID TODAY AND (WHY) IT MADE ME PROUD/HAPPY/ SURPRISED/UPSET

_____

_____

_____

_____

_____

MY ADVICE TO MY DAD

_____

_____

I WANT TO DO WITH MY DAD

_____

_____

_____

_____

FATHER

DATE:

TODAY I WANT TO SAY TO MY DAUGHTER

_____

_____

_____

_____

_____

WHAT MY DAUGHTER DID TODAY AND (WHY) IT MADE ME PROUD/HAPPY/ SURPRISED/UPSET

_____

_____

_____

_____

_____

MY ADVICE TO MY DAUGHTER

_____

_____

I WANT TO DO WITH MY DAUGHTER

_____

_____

_____

_____

DAUGHTER

DATE: _____

TODAY I WANT TO SAY TO MY DAD

_____

_____

_____

_____

WHAT MY DAD DID TODAY AND (WHY) IT MADE ME PROUD/HAPPY/ SURPRISED/UPSET

_____

_____

_____

_____

_____

MY ADVICE TO MY DAD

_____

_____

I WANT TO DO WITH MY DAD

_____

_____

_____

_____

FATHER

DATE:

TODAY I WANT TO SAY TO MY DAUGHTER

_____
_____
_____
_____
_____

WHAT MY DAUGHTER DID TODAY AND (WHY) IT MADE ME PROUD/HAPPY/ SURPRISED/UPSET

_____
_____
_____
_____
_____
_____

MY ADVICE TO MY DAUGHTER

_____
_____

I WANT TO DO WITH MY DAUGHTER

_____
_____
_____
_____

DAUGHTER

DATE:

TODAY I WANT TO SAY TO MY DAD

_____

_____

_____

_____

_____

WHAT MY DAD DID TODAY AND (WHY) IT MADE
ME PROUD/HAPPY/ SURPRISED/UPSET

_____

_____

_____

_____

_____

MY ADVICE TO MY DAD

_____

_____

I WANT TO DO WITH MY DAD

_____

_____

_____

_____

FATHER

DATE: _____

TODAY I WANT TO SAY TO MY DAUGHTER

_____

_____

_____

_____

WHAT MY DAUGHTER DID TODAY AND (WHY) IT MADE ME PROUD/HAPPY/ SURPRISED/UPSET

_____

_____

_____

_____

_____

MY ADVICE TO MY DAUGHTER

_____

_____

I WANT TO DO WITH MY DAUGHTER

_____

_____

_____

DAUGHTER

DATE:

TODAY I WANT TO SAY TO MY DAD

_____

_____

_____

_____

WHAT MY DAD DID TODAY AND (WHY) IT MADE ME PROUD/HAPPY/ SURPRISED/UPSET

_____

_____

_____

_____

_____

MY ADVICE TO MY DAD

_____

_____

I WANT TO DO WITH MY DAD

_____

_____

_____

FATHER

DATE:

TODAY I WANT TO SAY TO MY DAUGHTER

_____

_____

_____

_____

_____

WHAT MY DAUGHTER DID TODAY AND (WHY) IT MADE ME PROUD/HAPPY/ SURPRISED/UPSET

_____

_____

_____

_____

_____

MY ADVICE TO MY DAUGHTER

_____

_____

I WANT TO DO WITH MY DAUGHTER

_____

_____

_____

_____

DAUGHTER

DATE:

TODAY I WANT TO SAY TO MY DAD

_____

_____

_____

_____

WHAT MY DAD DID TODAY AND (WHY) IT MADE ME PROUD/HAPPY/ SURPRISED/UPSET

_____

_____

_____

_____

MY ADVICE TO MY DAD

_____

_____

I WANT TO DO WITH MY DAD

_____

_____

_____

FATHER

DATE: _____

TODAY I WANT TO SAY TO MY DAUGHTER

_____
_____
_____
_____
_____

WHAT MY DAUGHTER DID TODAY AND (WHY) IT MADE ME PROUD/HAPPY/ SURPRISED/UPSET

_____
_____
_____
_____
_____
_____

MY ADVICE TO MY DAUGHTER

_____
_____

I WANT TO DO WITH MY DAUGHTER

_____
_____
_____

DAUGHTER

DATE: _____

TODAY I WANT TO SAY TO MY DAD

_____
_____
_____
_____
_____

WHAT MY DAD DID TODAY AND (WHY) IT MADE ME PROUD/HAPPY/ SURPRISED/UPSET

_____
_____
_____
_____
_____

MY ADVICE TO MY DAD

_____
_____

I WANT TO DO WITH MY DAD

_____
_____
_____

FATHER

DATE:

TODAY I WANT TO SAY TO MY DAUGHTER

_____

_____

_____

_____

_____

WHAT MY DAUGHTER DID TODAY AND (WHY) IT MADE ME PROUD/HAPPY/ SURPRISED/UPSET

_____

_____

_____

_____

_____

MY ADVICE TO MY DAUGHTER

_____

_____

I WANT TO DO WITH MY DAUGHTER

_____

_____

_____

DAUGHTER

DATE: _____

TODAY I WANT TO SAY TO MY DAD

_____

_____

_____

_____

WHAT MY DAD DID TODAY AND (WHY) IT MADE ME PROUD/HAPPY/ SURPRISED/UPSET

_____

_____

_____

_____

_____

MY ADVICE TO MY DAD

_____

_____

I WANT TO DO WITH MY DAD

_____

_____

_____

_____

FATHER

DATE:

TODAY I WANT TO SAY TO MY DAUGHTER

_____
_____
_____
_____
_____

WHAT MY DAUGHTER DID TODAY AND (WHY) IT
MADE ME PROUD/HAPPY/ SURPRISED/UPSET

_____
_____
_____
_____
_____

MY ADVICE TO MY DAUGHTER

_____
_____

I WANT TO DO WITH MY DAUGHTER

_____
_____
_____

DAUGHTER

DATE: _____

TODAY I WANT TO SAY TO MY DAD

_____

_____

_____

_____

WHAT MY DAD DID TODAY AND (WHY) IT MADE ME PROUD/HAPPY/ SURPRISED/UPSET

_____

_____

_____

_____

_____

MY ADVICE TO MY DAD

_____

_____

I WANT TO DO WITH MY DAD

_____

_____

_____

_____

FATHER

DATE:

TODAY I WANT TO SAY TO MY DAUGHTER

_____
_____
_____
_____
_____

WHAT MY DAUGHTER DID TODAY AND (WHY) IT MADE ME PROUD/HAPPY/ SURPRISED/UPSET

_____
_____
_____
_____
_____
_____

MY ADVICE TO MY DAUGHTER

_____
_____

I WANT TO DO WITH MY DAUGHTER

_____
_____
_____
_____

DAUGHTER

DATE:

TODAY I WANT TO SAY TO MY DAD

_____

_____

_____

_____

WHAT MY DAD DID TODAY AND (WHY) IT MADE ME PROUD/HAPPY/ SURPRISED/UPSET

_____

_____

_____

_____

MY ADVICE TO MY DAD

_____

_____

I WANT TO DO WITH MY DAD

_____

_____

_____

_____

FATHER

DATE:

TODAY I WANT TO SAY TO MY DAUGHTER

_____

_____

_____

_____

_____

WHAT MY DAUGHTER DID TODAY AND (WHY) IT MADE ME PROUD/HAPPY/ SURPRISED/UPSET

_____

_____

_____

_____

_____

_____

MY ADVICE TO MY DAUGHTER

_____

_____

I WANT TO DO WITH MY DAUGHTER

_____

_____

_____

_____

DAUGHTER

DATE:

TODAY I WANT TO SAY TO MY DAD

_____
_____
_____
_____
_____

WHAT MY DAD DID TODAY AND (WHY) IT MADE ME PROUD/HAPPY/ SURPRISED/UPSET

_____
_____
_____
_____
_____

MY ADVICE TO MY DAD

_____
_____

I WANT TO DO WITH MY DAD

_____
_____
_____
_____

FATHER

DATE:

TODAY I WANT TO SAY TO MY DAUGHTER

_____
_____
_____
_____
_____

WHAT MY DAUGHTER DID TODAY AND (WHY) IT MADE ME PROUD/HAPPY/ SURPRISED/UPSET

_____
_____
_____
_____
_____

MY ADVICE TO MY DAUGHTER

_____
_____

I WANT TO DO WITH MY DAUGHTER

_____
_____
_____
_____

DAUGHTER

DATE:

TODAY I WANT TO SAY TO MY DAD

_____

_____

_____

_____

WHAT MY DAD DID TODAY AND (WHY) IT MADE ME PROUD/HAPPY/ SURPRISED/UPSET

_____

_____

_____

_____

MY ADVICE TO MY DAD

_____

_____

I WANT TO DO WITH MY DAD

_____

_____

_____

FATHER

<u>DATE:</u>

TODAY I WANT TO SAY TO MY DAUGHTER

_____
_____
_____
_____
_____

WHAT MY DAUGHTER DID TODAY AND (WHY) IT MADE ME PROUD/HAPPY/ SURPRISED/UPSET

_____
_____
_____
_____
_____

MY ADVICE TO MY DAUGHTER

_____
_____

I WANT TO DO WITH MY DAUGHTER

_____
_____
_____
_____

DAUGHTER

DATE:

TODAY I WANT TO SAY TO MY DAD

_____

_____

_____

_____

WHAT MY DAD DID TODAY AND (WHY) IT MADE ME PROUD/HAPPY/ SURPRISED/UPSET

_____

_____

_____

_____

_____

MY ADVICE TO MY DAD

_____

_____

I WANT TO DO WITH MY DAD

_____

_____

_____

_____

FATHER

DATE:

TODAY I WANT TO SAY TO MY DAUGHTER

_____

_____

_____

_____

_____

WHAT MY DAUGHTER DID TODAY AND (WHY) IT MADE ME PROUD/HAPPY/ SURPRISED/UPSET

_____

_____

_____

_____

_____

MY ADVICE TO MY DAUGHTER

_____

_____

I WANT TO DO WITH MY DAUGHTER

_____

_____

_____

DAUGHTER

DATE:

TODAY I WANT TO SAY TO MY DAD

_____

_____

_____

_____

WHAT MY DAD DID TODAY AND (WHY) IT MADE ME PROUD/HAPPY/ SURPRISED/UPSET

_____

_____

_____

_____

MY ADVICE TO MY DAD

_____

_____

I WANT TO DO WITH MY DAD

_____

_____

_____

FATHER

DATE:

TODAY I WANT TO SAY TO MY DAUGHTER

_____
_____
_____
_____
_____
_____

WHAT MY DAUGHTER DID TODAY AND (WHY) IT MADE ME PROUD/HAPPY/ SURPRISED/UPSET

_____
_____
_____
_____
_____
_____

MY ADVICE TO MY DAUGHTER

_____
_____

I WANT TO DO WITH MY DAUGHTER

_____
_____
_____
_____

DAUGHTER

DATE:

TODAY I WANT TO SAY TO MY DAD

_____

_____

_____

_____

WHAT MY DAD DID TODAY AND (WHY) IT MADE ME PROUD/HAPPY/ SURPRISED/UPSET

_____

_____

_____

_____

_____

MY ADVICE TO MY DAD

_____

_____

I WANT TO DO WITH MY DAD

_____

_____

_____

FATHER

DATE:

TODAY I WANT TO SAY TO MY DAUGHTER

_____

_____

_____

_____

_____

WHAT MY DAUGHTER DID TODAY AND (WHY) IT MADE ME PROUD/HAPPY/ SURPRISED/UPSET

_____

_____

_____

_____

_____

_____

MY ADVICE TO MY DAUGHTER

_____

_____

I WANT TO DO WITH MY DAUGHTER

_____

_____

_____

DAUGHTER

DATE:

TODAY I WANT TO SAY TO MY DAD

_____

_____

_____

_____

WHAT MY DAD DID TODAY AND (WHY) IT MADE ME PROUD/HAPPY/ SURPRISED/UPSET

_____

_____

_____

_____

_____

MY ADVICE TO MY DAD

_____

_____

I WANT TO DO WITH MY DAD

_____

_____

_____

FATHER

DATE:

TODAY I WANT TO SAY TO MY DAUGHTER

_____
_____
_____
_____
_____
_____

WHAT MY DAUGHTER DID TODAY AND (WHY) IT MADE ME PROUD/HAPPY/ SURPRISED/UPSET

_____
_____
_____
_____
_____
_____

MY ADVICE TO MY DAUGHTER

_____
_____

I WANT TO DO WITH MY DAUGHTER

_____
_____
_____
_____

DAUGHTER

DATE:

TODAY I WANT TO SAY TO MY DAD

_____

_____

_____

_____

_____

WHAT MY DAD DID TODAY AND (WHY) IT MADE ME PROUD/HAPPY/ SURPRISED/UPSET

_____

_____

_____

_____

_____

MY ADVICE TO MY DAD

_____

_____

I WANT TO DO WITH MY DAD

_____

_____

_____

_____

FATHER

DATE:

TODAY I WANT TO SAY TO MY DAUGHTER

_____
_____
_____
_____

WHAT MY DAUGHTER DID TODAY AND (WHY) IT MADE ME PROUD/HAPPY/ SURPRISED/UPSET

_____
_____
_____
_____
_____
_____

MY ADVICE TO MY DAUGHTER

_____
_____

I WANT TO DO WITH MY DAUGHTER

_____
_____
_____
_____

DAUGHTER

DATE:

TODAY I WANT TO SAY TO MY DAD

_____

_____

_____

_____

WHAT MY DAD DID TODAY AND (WHY) IT MADE ME PROUD/HAPPY/ SURPRISED/UPSET

_____

_____

_____

_____

_____

MY ADVICE TO MY DAD

_____

_____

I WANT TO DO WITH MY DAD

_____

_____

_____

FATHER

DATE:

TODAY I WANT TO SAY TO MY DAUGHTER

_____

_____

_____

_____

_____

WHAT MY DAUGHTER DID TODAY AND (WHY) IT MADE ME PROUD/HAPPY/ SURPRISED/UPSET

_____

_____

_____

_____

_____

MY ADVICE TO MY DAUGHTER

_____

_____

I WANT TO DO WITH MY DAUGHTER

_____

_____

_____

DAUGHTER

DATE:

TODAY I WANT TO SAY TO MY DAD

_____

_____

_____

_____

WHAT MY DAD DID TODAY AND (WHY) IT MADE ME PROUD/HAPPY/ SURPRISED/UPSET

_____

_____

_____

_____

MY ADVICE TO MY DAD

_____

_____

I WANT TO DO WITH MY DAD

_____

_____

_____

FATHER

DATE:

TODAY I WANT TO SAY TO MY DAUGHTER

_____
_____
_____
_____
_____

WHAT MY DAUGHTER DID TODAY AND (WHY) IT MADE ME PROUD/HAPPY/ SURPRISED/UPSET

_____
_____
_____
_____
_____

MY ADVICE TO MY DAUGHTER

_____
_____

I WANT TO DO WITH MY DAUGHTER

_____
_____
_____
_____

DAUGHTER

DATE: _____

TODAY I WANT TO SAY TO MY DAD

_____

_____

_____

_____

WHAT MY DAD DID TODAY AND (WHY) IT MADE ME PROUD/HAPPY/ SURPRISED/UPSET

_____

_____

_____

_____

MY ADVICE TO MY DAD

_____

_____

I WANT TO DO WITH MY DAD

_____

_____

_____

_____

FATHER

DATE:

TODAY I WANT TO SAY TO MY DAUGHTER

_____

_____

_____

_____

_____

_____

WHAT MY DAUGHTER DID TODAY AND (WHY) IT MADE ME PROUD/HAPPY/ SURPRISED/UPSET

_____

_____

_____

_____

_____

_____

_____

_____

MY ADVICE TO MY DAUGHTER

_____

_____

_____

I WANT TO DO WITH MY DAUGHTER

_____

_____

_____

_____

_____

DAUGHTER

DATE:

TODAY I WANT TO SAY TO MY DAD

_____

_____

_____

_____

_____

WHAT MY DAD DID TODAY AND (WHY) IT MADE ME PROUD/HAPPY/ SURPRISED/UPSET

_____

_____

_____

_____

_____

MY ADVICE TO MY DAD

_____

_____

I WANT TO DO WITH MY DAD

_____

_____

_____

_____

FATHER

DATE:

TODAY I WANT TO SAY TO MY DAUGHTER

_____
_____
_____
_____
_____

WHAT MY DAUGHTER DID TODAY AND (WHY) IT MADE ME PROUD/HAPPY/ SURPRISED/UPSET

_____
_____
_____
_____
_____

MY ADVICE TO MY DAUGHTER

_____
_____

I WANT TO DO WITH MY DAUGHTER

_____
_____
_____
_____

DAUGHTER

DATE:

TODAY I WANT TO SAY TO MY DAD

_____

_____

_____

_____

WHAT MY DAD DID TODAY AND (WHY) IT MADE ME PROUD/HAPPY/ SURPRISED/UPSET

_____

_____

_____

_____

_____

MY ADVICE TO MY DAD

_____

_____

I WANT TO DO WITH MY DAD

_____

_____

_____

_____

FATHER

DATE: _____

TODAY I WANT TO SAY TO MY DAUGHTER

_____

_____

_____

_____

WHAT MY DAUGHTER DID TODAY AND (WHY) IT MADE ME PROUD/HAPPY/ SURPRISED/UPSET

_____

_____

_____

_____

_____

_____

MY ADVICE TO MY DAUGHTER

_____

_____

I WANT TO DO WITH MY DAUGHTER

_____

_____

_____

DAUGHTER

DATE:

TODAY I WANT TO SAY TO MY DAD

_____

_____

_____

_____

WHAT MY DAD DID TODAY AND (WHY) IT MADE ME PROUD/HAPPY/ SURPRISED/UPSET

_____

_____

_____

_____

_____

MY ADVICE TO MY DAD

_____

_____

I WANT TO DO WITH MY DAD

_____

_____

_____

_____

FATHER

DATE:

TODAY I WANT TO SAY TO MY DAUGHTER

_____
_____
_____
_____
_____

WHAT MY DAUGHTER DID TODAY AND (WHY) IT MADE ME PROUD/HAPPY/ SURPRISED/UPSET

_____
_____
_____
_____
_____
_____

MY ADVICE TO MY DAUGHTER

_____
_____

I WANT TO DO WITH MY DAUGHTER

_____
_____
_____
_____

DAUGHTER

DATE:

TODAY I WANT TO SAY TO MY DAD

_____

_____

_____

_____

WHAT MY DAD DID TODAY AND (WHY) IT MADE ME PROUD/HAPPY/ SURPRISED/UPSET

_____

_____

_____

_____

MY ADVICE TO MY DAD

_____

_____

I WANT TO DO WITH MY DAD

_____

_____

_____

FATHER

DATE:

TODAY I WANT TO SAY TO MY DAUGHTER

_____

_____

_____

_____

WHAT MY DAUGHTER DID TODAY AND (WHY) IT MADE ME PROUD/HAPPY/ SURPRISED/UPSET

_____

_____

_____

_____

MY ADVICE TO MY DAUGHTER

_____

_____

I WANT TO DO WITH MY DAUGHTER

_____

_____

_____

DAUGHTER

DATE: _____

TODAY I WANT TO SAY TO MY DAD

_____

_____

_____

_____

WHAT MY DAD DID TODAY AND (WHY) IT MADE ME PROUD/HAPPY/ SURPRISED/UPSET

_____

_____

_____

_____

_____

MY ADVICE TO MY DAD

_____

_____

I WANT TO DO WITH MY DAD

_____

_____

_____

_____

FATHER

DATE:

TODAY I WANT TO SAY TO MY DAUGHTER

_____
_____
_____
_____
_____

WHAT MY DAUGHTER DID TODAY AND (WHY) IT MADE ME PROUD/HAPPY/ SURPRISED/UPSET

_____
_____
_____
_____
_____

MY ADVICE TO MY DAUGHTER

_____
_____

I WANT TO DO WITH MY DAUGHTER

_____
_____
_____

DAUGHTER

DATE: _____

TODAY I WANT TO SAY TO MY DAD

_____

_____

_____

_____

WHAT MY DAD DID TODAY AND (WHY) IT MADE ME PROUD/HAPPY/ SURPRISED/UPSET

_____

_____

_____

_____

MY ADVICE TO MY DAD

_____

_____

I WANT TO DO WITH MY DAD

_____

_____

_____

FATHER

DATE: _____

TODAY I WANT TO SAY TO MY DAUGHTER

_____

_____

_____

_____

WHAT MY DAUGHTER DID TODAY AND (WHY) IT MADE ME PROUD/HAPPY/ SURPRISED/UPSET

_____

_____

_____

_____

_____

MY ADVICE TO MY DAUGHTER

_____

_____

I WANT TO DO WITH MY DAUGHTER

_____

_____

_____

DAUGHTER

DATE:

TODAY I WANT TO SAY TO MY DAD

_____

_____

_____

_____

_____

WHAT MY DAD DID TODAY AND (WHY) IT MADE ME PROUD/HAPPY/ SURPRISED/UPSET

_____

_____

_____

_____

_____

_____

MY ADVICE TO MY DAD

_____

_____

I WANT TO DO WITH MY DAD

_____

_____

_____

_____

FATHER

DATE:

TODAY I WANT TO SAY TO MY DAUGHTER

_____
_____
_____
_____
_____

WHAT MY DAUGHTER DID TODAY AND (WHY) IT MADE ME PROUD/HAPPY/ SURPRISED/UPSET

_____
_____
_____
_____
_____
_____

MY ADVICE TO MY DAUGHTER

_____
_____

I WANT TO DO WITH MY DAUGHTER

_____
_____
_____
_____

DAUGHTER

DATE:

TODAY I WANT TO SAY TO MY DAD

_____

_____

_____

_____

WHAT MY DAD DID TODAY AND (WHY) IT MADE ME PROUD/HAPPY/ SURPRISED/UPSET

_____

_____

_____

_____

_____

MY ADVICE TO MY DAD

_____

_____

I WANT TO DO WITH MY DAD

_____

_____

_____

FATHER

DATE:

TODAY I WANT TO SAY TO MY DAUGHTER

_____

_____

_____

_____

WHAT MY DAUGHTER DID TODAY AND (WHY) IT MADE ME PROUD/HAPPY/ SURPRISED/UPSET

_____

_____

_____

_____

_____

MY ADVICE TO MY DAUGHTER

_____

_____

I WANT TO DO WITH MY DAUGHTER

_____

_____

_____

DAUGHTER

DATE: _____

TODAY I WANT TO SAY TO MY DAD

_____

_____

_____

_____

WHAT MY DAD DID TODAY AND (WHY) IT MADE ME PROUD/HAPPY/ SURPRISED/UPSET

_____

_____

_____

_____

_____

MY ADVICE TO MY DAD

_____

_____

I WANT TO DO WITH MY DAD

_____

_____

_____

_____

FATHER

DATE:

TODAY I WANT TO SAY TO MY DAUGHTER

_____
_____
_____
_____
_____

WHAT MY DAUGHTER DID TODAY AND (WHY) IT MADE ME PROUD/HAPPY/ SURPRISED/UPSET

_____
_____
_____
_____
_____

MY ADVICE TO MY DAUGHTER

_____
_____

I WANT TO DO WITH MY DAUGHTER

_____
_____
_____
_____

DAUGHTER

DATE:

TODAY I WANT TO SAY TO MY DAD

_____
_____
_____
_____

WHAT MY DAD DID TODAY AND (WHY) IT MADE ME PROUD/HAPPY/ SURPRISED/UPSET

_____
_____
_____
_____
_____

MY ADVICE TO MY DAD

_____
_____

I WANT TO DO WITH MY DAD

_____
_____
_____
_____

FATHER

DATE:

TODAY I WANT TO SAY TO MY DAUGHTER

_____
_____
_____
_____
_____

WHAT MY DAUGHTER DID TODAY AND (WHY) IT MADE ME PROUD/HAPPY/ SURPRISED/UPSET

_____
_____
_____
_____
_____

MY ADVICE TO MY DAUGHTER

_____
_____

I WANT TO DO WITH MY DAUGHTER

_____
_____
_____

DAUGHTER

DATE: _____

TODAY I WANT TO SAY TO MY DAD

_____

_____

_____

_____

_____

WHAT MY DAD DID TODAY AND (WHY) IT MADE ME PROUD/HAPPY/ SURPRISED/UPSET

_____

_____

_____

_____

_____

MY ADVICE TO MY DAD

_____

_____

I WANT TO DO WITH MY DAD

_____

_____

_____

_____

FATHER

DATE:

TODAY I WANT TO SAY TO MY DAUGHTER

_____

_____

_____

_____

_____

_____

WHAT MY DAUGHTER DID TODAY AND (WHY) IT MADE ME PROUD/HAPPY/ SURPRISED/UPSET

_____

_____

_____

_____

_____

_____

MY ADVICE TO MY DAUGHTER

_____

_____

I WANT TO DO WITH MY DAUGHTER

_____

_____

_____

_____

DAUGHTER

<u>DATE:</u>

TODAY I WANT TO SAY TO MY DAD

_____

_____

_____

_____

WHAT MY DAD DID TODAY AND (WHY) IT MADE ME PROUD/HAPPY/ SURPRISED/UPSET

_____

_____

_____

_____

MY ADVICE TO MY DAD

_____

_____

I WANT TO DO WITH MY DAD

_____

_____

_____

FATHER

DATE: _____

TODAY I WANT TO SAY TO MY DAUGHTER

_____

_____

_____

_____

WHAT MY DAUGHTER DID TODAY AND (WHY) IT MADE ME PROUD/HAPPY/ SURPRISED/UPSET

_____

_____

_____

_____

_____

MY ADVICE TO MY DAUGHTER

_____

_____

I WANT TO DO WITH MY DAUGHTER

_____

_____

_____

_____

DAUGHTER

DATE:

TODAY I WANT TO SAY TO MY DAD

_____

_____

_____

_____

_____

WHAT MY DAD DID TODAY AND (WHY) IT MADE ME PROUD/HAPPY/ SURPRISED/UPSET

_____

_____

_____

_____

_____

_____

MY ADVICE TO MY DAD

_____

_____

I WANT TO DO WITH MY DAD

_____

_____

_____

_____

FATHER

TODAY I WANT TO SAY TO MY DAUGHTER

_____
_____
_____
_____
_____
_____

WHAT MY DAUGHTER DID TODAY AND (WHY) IT MADE ME PROUD/HAPPY/ SURPRISED/UPSET

_____
_____
_____
_____
_____
_____
_____
_____

MY ADVICE TO MY DAUGHTER

_____
_____

I WANT TO DO WITH MY DAUGHTER

_____
_____
_____
_____

DAUGHTER

DATE:

TODAY I WANT TO SAY TO MY DAD

_____
_____
_____
_____

WHAT MY DAD DID TODAY AND (WHY) IT MADE ME PROUD/HAPPY/ SURPRISED/UPSET

_____
_____
_____
_____

MY ADVICE TO MY DAD

_____
_____

I WANT TO DO WITH MY DAD

_____
_____
_____
_____

FATHER

DATE:

TODAY I WANT TO SAY TO MY DAUGHTER

_____

_____

_____

_____

_____

WHAT MY DAUGHTER DID TODAY AND (WHY) IT MADE ME PROUD/HAPPY/ SURPRISED/UPSET

_____

_____

_____

_____

_____

MY ADVICE TO MY DAUGHTER

_____

_____

I WANT TO DO WITH MY DAUGHTER

_____

_____

_____

_____

DAUGHTER

DATE:

TODAY I WANT TO SAY TO MY DAD

_____

_____

_____

_____

WHAT MY DAD DID TODAY AND (WHY) IT MADE ME PROUD/HAPPY/ SURPRISED/UPSET

_____

_____

_____

_____

_____

MY ADVICE TO MY DAD

_____

_____

I WANT TO DO WITH MY DAD

_____

_____

_____

_____

FATHER

DATE:

TODAY I WANT TO SAY TO MY DAUGHTER

_____
_____
_____
_____

WHAT MY DAUGHTER DID TODAY AND (WHY) IT MADE ME PROUD/HAPPY/ SURPRISED/UPSET

_____
_____
_____
_____
_____
_____

MY ADVICE TO MY DAUGHTER

_____
_____

I WANT TO DO WITH MY DAUGHTER

_____
_____
_____
_____

DAUGHTER

DATE: _____

TODAY I WANT TO SAY TO MY DAD

_____

_____

_____

_____

WHAT MY DAD DID TODAY AND (WHY) IT MADE ME PROUD/HAPPY/ SURPRISED/UPSET

_____

_____

_____

_____

MY ADVICE TO MY DAD

_____

_____

I WANT TO DO WITH MY DAD

_____

_____

_____

_____

FATHER

DATE:

TODAY I WANT TO SAY TO MY DAUGHTER

_____
_____
_____
_____
_____

WHAT MY DAUGHTER DID TODAY AND (WHY) IT MADE ME PROUD/HAPPY/ SURPRISED/UPSET

_____
_____
_____
_____
_____
_____
_____

MY ADVICE TO MY DAUGHTER

_____
_____

I WANT TO DO WITH MY DAUGHTER

_____
_____
_____
_____

DAUGHTER

DATE:

TODAY I WANT TO SAY TO MY DAD

_____

_____

_____

_____

WHAT MY DAD DID TODAY AND (WHY) IT MADE ME PROUD/HAPPY/ SURPRISED/UPSET

_____

_____

_____

_____

_____

MY ADVICE TO MY DAD

_____

_____

I WANT TO DO WITH MY DAD

_____

_____

_____

FATHER

DATE: _____

TODAY I WANT TO SAY TO MY DAUGHTER

_____
_____
_____
_____
_____

WHAT MY DAUGHTER DID TODAY AND (WHY) IT MADE ME PROUD/HAPPY/ SURPRISED/UPSET

_____
_____
_____
_____
_____
_____

MY ADVICE TO MY DAUGHTER

_____
_____

I WANT TO DO WITH MY DAUGHTER

_____
_____
_____
_____

DAUGHTER

DATE:

TODAY I WANT TO SAY TO MY DAD

_____

_____

_____

_____

WHAT MY DAD DID TODAY AND (WHY) IT MADE ME PROUD/HAPPY/ SURPRISED/UPSET

_____

_____

_____

_____

MY ADVICE TO MY DAD

_____

_____

I WANT TO DO WITH MY DAD

_____

_____

_____

FATHER

DATE:

TODAY I WANT TO SAY TO MY DAUGHTER

_____

_____

_____

_____

WHAT MY DAUGHTER DID TODAY AND (WHY) IT MADE ME PROUD/HAPPY/ SURPRISED/UPSET

_____

_____

_____

_____

_____

MY ADVICE TO MY DAUGHTER

_____

_____

I WANT TO DO WITH MY DAUGHTER

_____

_____

_____

DAUGHTER

DATE:

TODAY I WANT TO SAY TO MY DAD

_____
_____
_____
_____
_____

WHAT MY DAD DID TODAY AND (WHY) IT MADE
ME PROUD/HAPPY/ SURPRISED/UPSET

_____
_____
_____
_____
_____

MY ADVICE TO MY DAD

_____
_____

I WANT TO DO WITH MY DAD

_____
_____
_____
_____

FATHER

DATE:

TODAY I WANT TO SAY TO MY DAUGHTER

_____
_____
_____
_____
_____

WHAT MY DAUGHTER DID TODAY AND (WHY) IT MADE ME PROUD/HAPPY/ SURPRISED/UPSET

_____
_____
_____
_____
_____
_____

MY ADVICE TO MY DAUGHTER

_____
_____
_____

I WANT TO DO WITH MY DAUGHTER

_____
_____
_____
_____

DAUGHTER

DATE: _____

TODAY I WANT TO SAY TO MY DAD

_____

_____

_____

_____

WHAT MY DAD DID TODAY AND (WHY) IT MADE ME PROUD/HAPPY/ SURPRISED/UPSET

_____

_____

_____

_____

_____

MY ADVICE TO MY DAD

_____

_____

I WANT TO DO WITH MY DAD

_____

_____

_____

_____

FATHER

DATE:

TODAY I WANT TO SAY TO MY DAUGHTER

_____

_____

_____

_____

_____

WHAT MY DAUGHTER DID TODAY AND (WHY) IT MADE ME PROUD/HAPPY/ SURPRISED/UPSET

_____

_____

_____

_____

_____

MY ADVICE TO MY DAUGHTER

_____

_____

I WANT TO DO WITH MY DAUGHTER

_____

_____

_____

DAUGHTER

DATE:

TODAY I WANT TO SAY TO MY DAD

_____

_____

_____

_____

WHAT MY DAD DID TODAY AND (WHY) IT MADE ME PROUD/HAPPY/ SURPRISED/UPSET

_____

_____

_____

_____

_____

MY ADVICE TO MY DAD

_____

_____

I WANT TO DO WITH MY DAD

_____

_____

_____

FATHER

DATE: _____

TODAY I WANT TO SAY TO MY DAUGHTER

_____

_____

_____

_____

WHAT MY DAUGHTER DID TODAY AND (WHY) IT MADE ME PROUD/HAPPY/ SURPRISED/UPSET

_____

_____

_____

_____

_____

MY ADVICE TO MY DAUGHTER

_____

_____

I WANT TO DO WITH MY DAUGHTER

_____

_____

_____

_____

DAUGHTER

DATE:

TODAY I WANT TO SAY TO MY DAD

_____

_____

_____

_____

WHAT MY DAD DID TODAY AND (WHY) IT MADE ME PROUD/HAPPY/ SURPRISED/UPSET

_____

_____

_____

_____

MY ADVICE TO MY DAD

_____

_____

I WANT TO DO WITH MY DAD

_____

_____

_____

FATHER

DATE: _____

TODAY I WANT TO SAY TO MY DAUGHTER

_____

_____

_____

_____

_____

WHAT MY DAUGHTER DID TODAY AND (WHY) IT
MADE ME PROUD/HAPPY/ SURPRISED/UPSET

_____

_____

_____

_____

_____

MY ADVICE TO MY DAUGHTER

_____

_____

I WANT TO DO WITH MY DAUGHTER

_____

_____

_____

_____

DAUGHTER

DATE:

TODAY I WANT TO SAY TO MY DAD

_____

_____

_____

_____

WHAT MY DAD DID TODAY AND (WHY) IT MADE
ME PROUD/HAPPY/ SURPRISED/UPSET

_____

_____

_____

_____

_____

MY ADVICE TO MY DAD

_____

_____

I WANT TO DO WITH MY DAD

_____

_____

_____

FATHER

DATE: _____

TODAY I WANT TO SAY TO MY DAUGHTER

_____

_____

_____

_____

_____

WHAT MY DAUGHTER DID TODAY AND (WHY) IT MADE ME PROUD/HAPPY/ SURPRISED/UPSET

_____

_____

_____

_____

_____

MY ADVICE TO MY DAUGHTER

_____

_____

I WANT TO DO WITH MY DAUGHTER

_____

_____

_____

DAUGHTER

DATE:

TODAY I WANT TO SAY TO MY DAD

_____

_____

_____

_____

WHAT MY DAD DID TODAY AND (WHY) IT MADE ME PROUD/HAPPY/ SURPRISED/UPSET

_____

_____

_____

_____

MY ADVICE TO MY DAD

_____

_____

I WANT TO DO WITH MY DAD

_____

_____

_____

FATHER

DATE:

TODAY I WANT TO SAY TO MY DAUGHTER

_____

_____

_____

_____

_____

WHAT MY DAUGHTER DID TODAY AND (WHY) IT MADE ME PROUD/HAPPY/ SURPRISED/UPSET

_____

_____

_____

_____

_____

_____

MY ADVICE TO MY DAUGHTER

_____

_____

_____

I WANT TO DO WITH MY DAUGHTER

_____

_____

_____

_____

DAUGHTER

DATE:

TODAY I WANT TO SAY TO MY DAD

_____

_____

_____

_____

WHAT MY DAD DID TODAY AND (WHY) IT MADE ME PROUD/HAPPY/ SURPRISED/UPSET

_____

_____

_____

_____

_____

MY ADVICE TO MY DAD

_____

_____

I WANT TO DO WITH MY DAD

_____

_____

_____

FATHER

DATE:

TODAY I WANT TO SAY TO MY DAUGHTER

_____
_____
_____
_____
_____

WHAT MY DAUGHTER DID TODAY AND (WHY) IT MADE ME PROUD/HAPPY/ SURPRISED/UPSET

_____
_____
_____
_____
_____
_____

MY ADVICE TO MY DAUGHTER

_____
_____

I WANT TO DO WITH MY DAUGHTER

_____
_____
_____

DAUGHTER

DATE:

TODAY I WANT TO SAY TO MY DAD

_____

_____

_____

_____

WHAT MY DAD DID TODAY AND (WHY) IT MADE ME PROUD/HAPPY/ SURPRISED/UPSET

_____

_____

_____

_____

MY ADVICE TO MY DAD

_____

_____

I WANT TO DO WITH MY DAD

_____

_____

_____

_____

FATHER

DATE:

TODAY I WANT TO SAY TO MY DAUGHTER

_____

_____

_____

_____

_____

WHAT MY DAUGHTER DID TODAY AND (WHY) IT MADE ME PROUD/HAPPY/ SURPRISED/UPSET

_____

_____

_____

_____

_____

MY ADVICE TO MY DAUGHTER

_____

_____

I WANT TO DO WITH MY DAUGHTER

_____

_____

_____

_____

DAUGHTER

DATE:

TODAY I WANT TO SAY TO MY DAD

_____

_____

_____

_____

WHAT MY DAD DID TODAY AND (WHY) IT MADE ME PROUD/HAPPY/ SURPRISED/UPSET

_____

_____

_____

_____

_____

MY ADVICE TO MY DAD

_____

_____

I WANT TO DO WITH MY DAD

_____

_____

_____

FATHER

DATE:

TODAY I WANT TO SAY TO MY DAUGHTER

_____

_____

_____

_____

_____

WHAT MY DAUGHTER DID TODAY AND (WHY) IT MADE ME PROUD/HAPPY/ SURPRISED/UPSET

_____

_____

_____

_____

_____

MY ADVICE TO MY DAUGHTER

_____

_____

I WANT TO DO WITH MY DAUGHTER

_____

_____

_____

_____

DAUGHTER

DATE:

TODAY I WANT TO SAY TO MY DAD

_____

_____

_____

_____

WHAT MY DAD DID TODAY AND (WHY) IT MADE ME PROUD/HAPPY/ SURPRISED/UPSET

_____

_____

_____

_____

_____

MY ADVICE TO MY DAD

_____

_____

I WANT TO DO WITH MY DAD

_____

_____

_____

FATHER

DATE:

TODAY I WANT TO SAY TO MY DAUGHTER

_____

_____

_____

_____

_____

WHAT MY DAUGHTER DID TODAY AND (WHY) IT MADE ME PROUD/HAPPY/ SURPRISED/UPSET

_____

_____

_____

_____

_____

MY ADVICE TO MY DAUGHTER

_____

_____

I WANT TO DO WITH MY DAUGHTER

_____

_____

_____

_____

DAUGHTER

DATE: _____

TODAY I WANT TO SAY TO MY DAD

_____

_____

_____

_____

WHAT MY DAD DID TODAY AND (WHY) IT MADE ME PROUD/HAPPY/ SURPRISED/UPSET

_____

_____

_____

_____

_____

MY ADVICE TO MY DAD

_____

_____

I WANT TO DO WITH MY DAD

_____

_____

_____

_____

FATHER

DATE: _____

TODAY I WANT TO SAY TO MY DAUGHTER

_____

_____

_____

_____

_____

WHAT MY DAUGHTER DID TODAY AND (WHY) IT MADE ME PROUD/HAPPY/ SURPRISED/UPSET

_____

_____

_____

_____

_____

MY ADVICE TO MY DAUGHTER

_____

_____

I WANT TO DO WITH MY DAUGHTER

_____

_____

_____

DAUGHTER

DATE:

TODAY I WANT TO SAY TO MY DAD

_____

_____

_____

_____

WHAT MY DAD DID TODAY AND (WHY) IT MADE ME PROUD/HAPPY/ SURPRISED/UPSET

_____

_____

_____

_____

_____

MY ADVICE TO MY DAD

_____

_____

I WANT TO DO WITH MY DAD

_____

_____

_____

FATHER

DATE:

TODAY I WANT TO SAY TO MY DAUGHTER

_____

_____

_____

_____

_____

WHAT MY DAUGHTER DID TODAY AND (WHY) IT MADE ME PROUD/HAPPY/ SURPRISED/UPSET

_____

_____

_____

_____

_____

_____

MY ADVICE TO MY DAUGHTER

_____

_____

I WANT TO DO WITH MY DAUGHTER

_____

_____

_____

_____

DAUGHTER

DATE:

TODAY I WANT TO SAY TO MY DAD

_____

_____

_____

_____

_____

WHAT MY DAD DID TODAY AND (WHY) IT MADE
ME PROUD/HAPPY/ SURPRISED/UPSET

_____

_____

_____

_____

_____

_____

MY ADVICE TO MY DAD

_____

_____

I WANT TO DO WITH MY DAD

_____

_____

_____

_____

FATHER

DATE: _____

TODAY I WANT TO SAY TO MY DAUGHTER

_____

_____

_____

_____

_____

WHAT MY DAUGHTER DID TODAY AND (WHY) IT MADE ME PROUD/HAPPY/ SURPRISED/UPSET

_____

_____

_____

_____

_____

MY ADVICE TO MY DAUGHTER

_____

_____

I WANT TO DO WITH MY DAUGHTER

_____

_____

_____

_____

DAUGHTER

DATE: _____

TODAY I WANT TO SAY TO MY DAD

_____

_____

_____

_____

WHAT MY DAD DID TODAY AND (WHY) IT MADE ME PROUD/HAPPY/ SURPRISED/UPSET

_____

_____

_____

_____

_____

MY ADVICE TO MY DAD

_____

_____

I WANT TO DO WITH MY DAD

_____

_____

_____

_____

FATHER

DATE:

TODAY I WANT TO SAY TO MY DAUGHTER

_____

_____

_____

_____

_____

WHAT MY DAUGHTER DID TODAY AND (WHY) IT MADE ME PROUD/HAPPY/ SURPRISED/UPSET

_____

_____

_____

_____

_____

MY ADVICE TO MY DAUGHTER

_____

_____

I WANT TO DO WITH MY DAUGHTER

_____

_____

_____

DAUGHTER

DATE:

TODAY I WANT TO SAY TO MY DAD

_____

_____

_____

_____

WHAT MY DAD DID TODAY AND (WHY) IT MADE ME PROUD/HAPPY/ SURPRISED/UPSET

_____

_____

_____

_____

_____

MY ADVICE TO MY DAD

_____

_____

I WANT TO DO WITH MY DAD

_____

_____

_____

_____

FATHER

DATE:

TODAY I WANT TO SAY TO MY DAUGHTER

_____
_____
_____
_____
_____

WHAT MY DAUGHTER DID TODAY AND (WHY) IT MADE ME PROUD/HAPPY/ SURPRISED/UPSET

_____
_____
_____
_____
_____

MY ADVICE TO MY DAUGHTER

_____
_____

I WANT TO DO WITH MY DAUGHTER

_____
_____
_____

DAUGHTER

DATE:

TODAY I WANT TO SAY TO MY DAD

_____
_____
_____
_____

WHAT MY DAD DID TODAY AND (WHY) IT MADE ME PROUD/HAPPY/ SURPRISED/UPSET

_____
_____
_____
_____

MY ADVICE TO MY DAD

_____
_____

I WANT TO DO WITH MY DAD

_____
_____
_____

FATHER

DATE:

TODAY I WANT TO SAY TO MY DAUGHTER

_____

_____

_____

_____

_____

WHAT MY DAUGHTER DID TODAY AND (WHY) IT MADE ME PROUD/HAPPY/ SURPRISED/UPSET

_____

_____

_____

_____

_____

MY ADVICE TO MY DAUGHTER

_____

_____

I WANT TO DO WITH MY DAUGHTER

_____

_____

_____

_____

DAUGHTER

DATE:

TODAY I WANT TO SAY TO MY DAD

_____

_____

_____

_____

WHAT MY DAD DID TODAY AND (WHY) IT MADE ME PROUD/HAPPY/ SURPRISED/UPSET

_____

_____

_____

_____

_____

MY ADVICE TO MY DAD

_____

_____

I WANT TO DO WITH MY DAD

_____

_____

_____

_____

FATHER

DATE:

TODAY I WANT TO SAY TO MY DAUGHTER

_____

_____

_____

_____

_____

WHAT MY DAUGHTER DID TODAY AND (WHY) IT MADE ME PROUD/HAPPY/ SURPRISED/UPSET

_____

_____

_____

_____

_____

MY ADVICE TO MY DAUGHTER

_____

_____

I WANT TO DO WITH MY DAUGHTER

_____

_____

_____

DAUGHTER

DATE:

TODAY I WANT TO SAY TO MY DAD

_____

_____

_____

_____

WHAT MY DAD DID TODAY AND (WHY) IT MADE ME PROUD/HAPPY/ SURPRISED/UPSET

_____

_____

_____

_____

_____

MY ADVICE TO MY DAD

_____

_____

I WANT TO DO WITH MY DAD

_____

_____

_____

FATHER

DATE: _____

TODAY I WANT TO SAY TO MY DAUGHTER

_____

_____

_____

_____

WHAT MY DAUGHTER DID TODAY AND (WHY) IT MADE ME PROUD/HAPPY/ SURPRISED/UPSET

_____

_____

_____

_____

_____

MY ADVICE TO MY DAUGHTER

_____

_____

I WANT TO DO WITH MY DAUGHTER

_____

_____

_____

DAUGHTER

DATE: _____

TODAY I WANT TO SAY TO MY DAD

_____

_____

_____

_____

WHAT MY DAD DID TODAY AND (WHY) IT MADE ME PROUD/HAPPY/ SURPRISED/UPSET

_____

_____

_____

_____

_____

MY ADVICE TO MY DAD

_____

_____

I WANT TO DO WITH MY DAD

_____

_____

_____

Made in United States
North Haven, CT
31 May 2022